THE WISDOM OF ST FRANCIS AND HIS
COMPANIONS

THE AUTHOR

Stephen Clissold, O.B.E., was born in 1913 and attended Salisbury Cathedral Choir School. He won an open scholarship to read Modern Languages at Oriel College, Oxford, where he first became interested in the writings of the mystics. He made his career in the British Council, serving in Denmark, Chile and Turkey, and with the Foreign Office. He is now retired and lives in Bayswater, London. He is the author of many books, including Latin America—A Cultural Outline; Latin America—New World, Third World; The Saints of South America; In Search of the Cid; Spain; The Wisdom of the Spanish Mystics *and a forthcoming biography of St Teresa. He is married with one daughter.*

THE WISDOM OF
ST FRANCIS AND HIS
COMPANIONS

COMPILED BY
STEPHEN CLISSOLD

A NEW DIRECTIONS BOOK

Manufactured in the United States of America
First published as New Directions Paperbook 477 in 1979 by
arrangement with Sheldon Press, London

Library of Congress Cataloging in Publication Data
Main entry under title:
The Wisdom of St Francis and his companions.
    (A New Directions Book)
    (Wisdom series)
    1. Francesco d'Assisi, Saint, 1182-1226.   2. Christian literature,
English.   I. Francesco d'Assisi, Saint, 1182-1226.   II. Clissold,
Stephen.   III. Series: Wisdom series (New York)
BX4700.F6W54   1978   230'.2   78-27504
ISBN 0-8112-0721-8

New Directions Books are published for James Laughlin
by New Directions Publishing Corporation,
80 Eighth Avenue, New York 10011

TABLE OF CONTENTS

THE WISDOM OF
ST FRANCIS AND HIS
COMPANIONS

*

STORIES AND SAYINGS

THE WISDOM OF
ST FRANCIS AND HIS COMPANIONS

IN ONE of those episodes of innocent and edifying
clowning in which the lives of the first Franciscans
abound, we read of Brother Masseo suddenly turning
to his companion and exclaiming: 'Why *you*? Why
you? Why *you*? You are neither handsome, well-born
nor particularly clever, yet the whole world seems to
be running after you!' Francis replied with his customary humility that it was precisely *because* he was such
a wretched, insignificant little fellow that God had
chosen to work through him, so that all might know
that whatever was accomplished was due to the divine
grace and power alone, and not wrongly ascribed to
the creature.

Today we may repeat Masseo's question in rather
different terms. How is it that in a world obsessed with
the need for 'development' and rising living standards
the life of a thirteenth-century merchant's son who
turned his back on such things and voluntarily chose
the most abject poverty holds such a fascination? Why
should we, who set such a high store on security and
the war against want, admire one who made himself a
tramp and a beggar, expected his companions to do
the same, and refused to have a cell, much less a
building, he could call his own? In an age which is
unashamedly materialistic and has rejected so many
traditional religious values, why does the personality
of the Little Poor Man of Assisi continue to attract?

Indeed, as our world recedes in spirit as well as in time from his own, his figure seems to grow ever more luminous and compelling.

Francis, it must be admitted, has sometimes been misunderstood or admired for the wrong reasons. He was something very much more, despite the undoubted power which he seems to have possessed over animals, than the rather mawkish animal-lover and patron saint of pets that he is sometimes portrayed. Nor, at the other extreme, did he remotely resemble the modish image of the revolutionary at odds with the political and ecclesiastical 'establishment' of his day. Francis propounded no new creed, offered no panaceas of his own, for the current social ills and wretchedness of which he was, however, keenly aware. He simply believed that the really important thing was to return to what he conceived to be the heart of the gospel teaching and live a life as near as possible to that of Jesus Christ. This meant, for himself, embracing voluntary poverty, humility, and obedience and devoting himself to prayer and service to others. And because he had a soul of extraordinary poetic sensibility as well as heroic compassion, he kindled an answering flame in others which continues to illumine us today. His originality lies in the completeness with which he imitated one greater than himself. His appeal remains topical because his message is timeless.

When Giovanni di Bernardone—known to contemporaries and posterity by his nickname of Francesco, 'Frenchy'—was born in the last quarter of the twelfth century, Christianity had been steadily permeating and reshaping the life of Europe for nearly a millennium. For the greater part of that time the faith originally professed by a small middle-eastern sect and neophites from the mixed population of the Roman empire had become the official creed of the rulers. Christianity had given medieval Europe its art and its learning and had moulded its laws, institutions, and the mores of its people. But it had lost much in the process. The Church was still the mother of saints; but it had also grown into a huge institution, corrupt and lax, absorbed in temporal affairs and ruled by prelates ambitious for power and wealth. The Italy in which Francis lived had become a battle-ground in the power-struggle between Emperor and Pope, and his native Assisi one of the numerous cities torn by civil strife between nobles and burghers, well-to-do citizens and the poor, and by rivalries with other neighbouring cities. They were bad times indeed.

It was not that no attempts at reform had been made. An energetic Pope would try to curb abuses by thundering out anathemas or by channelling warlike instincts into crusades. Saintly bishops or communities of pious, dedicated monks here and there irradiated examples of holy living. But the general picture was one of brutality, greed and immorality, not least amongst the tonsured ministers of the Church. It was still the age of faith, but of a faith often belied by evil practice. Beneath the ignorance and material misery of the people, the old religious fervour smouldered on, but wherever it was kindled into flame authority smelt real or fancied heresy and stamped it out.

In Francis's time the greatest challenge to the established Church was posed by zealots known as Cathars, 'the pure', or Albigensians, from the town of Albi in the south of France where they were particularly numerous. Their doctrine amounted to more than a heresy; it was a rival creed to Christianity itself and presented a view of the universe as governed by a dual deity, God and Satan, the former supreme in things spiritual, the latter in things material. The mass of the Cathars considered themselves free to live in this world, since it was Satan's domain, much as they pleased; eating, marrying, holding property, ignoring the sacraments and ceremonies of the Catholic Church, so long as they at least nominally joined the ranks of the 'Perfect', their priestly caste, before they died. The 'Perfect', in contrast, lived a life of extreme asceticism, withholding themselves from all contamination by Satan's handiwork. They practised strict celibacy and vegetarianism and possessed no property. Their austerity was in striking contrast to the prevailing worldliness of the Catholic clergy and won the respect of the people, whilst the free and easy life-style permitted to rank-and-file Cathars appealed strongly to temperaments which liked to have things both ways. Exhortation and threats proving unavailing, the Church only re-established her authority in the south of France in the wake of a bloody crusade. In north and central Italy, groups of Cathars, though persecuted, still persisted. Assisi itself for a time boasted a Cathar mayor.

Whilst the Pope was presiding over a Council called to consider the Cathar problem, he received in audience a former wool-merchant from Lyons called Peter Waldo. The merchant had been converted, given away all his property, and then started to exhort others to do likewise. The Bishop ordered him and his followers to stop preaching. Peter, in perplexity, asked the Pope how it could be wrong to tell others to live like the Apostles, who had had all things in common. After examining 'the Poor Men of Lyons' and finding that they had no wish to question the teaching or authority of the Church, the Pope allowed them to continue living in poverty, but not to preach since they were unlettered and might lead others into error. Some nevertheless ignored this prohibition; they were denounced as heretics and driven from their homes. The outcasts preached as they roamed and they multiplied rapidly. They now began to criticize the Church which had rejected them and proclaimed the need to return to Christ's own teaching and the poverty practised by his disciples. Other similar sects appeared, spreading their teaching as they went on pilgrimages or travelled on business. One of these was a brotherhood of Lombard cloth-workers known as the Humiliati, who worked in common and gave away to the poor whatever was not needed for their bare subsistence.

Pietro di Bernardone was a prosperous cloth-merchant who spent much of his time away from

Assisi. It seems likely that it was from one of his journeys that he brought back the bride from Provence who, in 1182, was to become Francis's mother. Hence the boy's nickname, and perhaps his lively nature, his delight in the French language and the courtly songs of the troubadours. His father does not seem to have been very religiously-minded, and he was certainly too prudent to allow himself to be infected with any Cathar taint, but Francis may have heard him talk of the Poor Men of Lyons or the Humiliati. Not that these devotees of poverty in any way influenced his extravagant and fun-loving youth. The merchant's son was always to the fore in the frolics of Assisi's gilded set, and less and less to be found behind his father's counter. He eagerly took his place too in the militia which sallied out against the city's powerful neighbour, Perugia, and even defeat, and a spell of captivity and illness, appeared unable at first to dampen his high spirits or lessen his confidence in the brilliant future which he predicted for himself. But back in Assisi once more, the old carefree life seemed to have lost its savour. He volunteered for another military escapade but turned back when it had scarcely begun. He no longer felt inclined to join in the merrymaking of his old companions.

Francis entered a spiritual crisis which was to last several years. The eyes of the gay-hearted young man were suddenly opened to the harsh reality of suffering —the suffering of the poor and maimed around him, and the suffering of the Christ who looked down from the cross above every church altar and each wayside shrine. This awareness was rendered the more painfully acute through Francis's extreme sensitivity to the natural beauty of the Umbrian countryside which was the setting for this scene of man's inhumanity to man and callous indifference towards God. Two extreme examples of wretchedness forced themselves upon his attention—the beggars and the lepers. To the first Francis had always opened his purse liberally, specially when alms were solicited for the love of God. The lepers, whose loathsome and dreaded disease condemned them to be shunned by society, made more exacting demands on his charity. Meeting a leper when he was out riding one day, Francis not only bestowed all his money on him, but forced himself to dismount and salute the outcast with the kiss of peace. From then on, the lepers became the special object of his loving care. Francis spent much time in the lazaretto tending them with his own hands and cheering them with his tender gaiety.

Imperceptibly, Francis was detaching himself from his old life, to the baffled indignation of the father who had made very different plans for his son. Francis had set his feet on a new path—but where would it lead? Beggars could be fed, and lepers tended; but how could the crucified Lord of all be served? One day, when kneeling in prayer in the tumble-down chapel of St Damian's, Francis was given the answer. The figure on the cross seemed to address him with the words: 'Francis, repair my church.' Trembling with joy and awe, Francis set about ful-filling the command with single-minded zeal. He had already learned something of the mason's craft through working with his fellow citizens to build a defensive wall for Assisi with the stones taken from the demolished feudal castle which had dominated their city. Now he went through the streets joyfully begging for gifts of stone which would enable him to build up God's ruined house. Many responded readily, astonished at the sight of Bernardone's son turned beggar and labourer.

Tension with his father came to a head when Francis, in his zeal to raise funds for his work, sold off a valuable consignment of Bernardone's wares and handed the proceeds to a priest. The case was brought before the bishop. Francis, in a dramatic gesture of renunciation, restored to his father not only the money but the very clothes he had been wearing, and declared that from then on he would look only to his heavenly father.

Francis was now a homeless wanderer and casual labourer. He had repaired not only St Damian's but one or two other little churches round Assisi. The command spoken to him from the cross he had carried out to the best of his ability and in the most literal manner. But what next? He had begun to preach—if preaching is not too grand a term for the simple and heartfelt appeals he would address to the curious bystanders at the street corners, bidding them turn from their sins and love God and their neighbours. Even such earnest little homilies had their dangers, as the Poor Men of Lyons had learned to their cost. Preaching was the privilege of the priests—though few now

10

availed themselves of it. How would they view the endeavours of this unconventional and unlettered lay-preacher? If there were some with the perception to see that his impassioned words contained the seeds of a movement of great spiritual renewal, how could they be sure that it would develop within the fold of the Church, revivifying its flagging energies, rather than run to waste in the wilderness of heresy?

Francis gradually came to understand that the injunction 'Repair my church' was to be taken in its wider, symbolic sense. The foundations had been laid by the master-builder and his disciples, living in absolute poverty, without material possessions of any kind, and entirely trusting in the Father's loving care to feed, clothe and provide for them as they went about his business. Francis felt called to imitate them as closely as possible, and so help to rebuild the spiritual church which had fallen into decay through caring for worldly things. He was not concerned with doctrines or established church practices, which he accepted without question. Nor with the administration of the Church, whose hierarchy he respected and obeyed implicitly. He was not even interested in learning, which he saw might well be more of a hindrance than a help to leading the life of austere simplicity, poverty, humility, prayer and service.

Francis passionately believed that the love of material possessions lay at the root of society's ills and of man's estrangement from his maker. Property implied the need for arms with which to defend it, and led to the struggle for power and prestige and to the chronic

11

warfare which was the scourge of his times. Once he had made himself a beggar for Christ, he experienced an extraordinary sense of freedom and joy. It was not poverty itself, but the deliberate acceptance of poverty for the love of Christ and his fellow-men, which he saw as the supreme good. He who thus willingly made himself poor became, in effect, the richest of men. Only then could he be fully aware of the mercies of a God who always provided for his children, and of the divine spark within each of them which charity could fan into a flame. Francis did not try to force his almost impossible ideal upon others who could not, or would not, choose the hard road of voluntary poverty. He did not denounce or try to convince by argument. It was enough to live out his own vocation to the full. And in time others came forward to join in the strange venture, and soon the trickle grew into a flood.

The first disciple whose name is known to us was Bernard of Quintavalle, a kindly, God-fearing merchant of Assisi, who offered Francis the hospitality of his house and was so moved by his guest's fervour that he gave away his considerable fortune in order to serve Lady Poverty. Bernard's friend Peter of Cataneo soon followed his example. He was an ecclesiastical lawyer and evidently a man of sound sense, for Francis later placed the governance of the new Order in his hands. Before long the little band was joined by the priest Sylvester, shamed by the sight of such apostolic fervour into abandoning his worldly concerns for a life of ascetic contemplation. Francis came to respect him greatly for his fervour in prayer. A much younger priest was Brother Leo, one of the most attractive of the companions in his whole-hearted devotion to Francis, who took him for his secretary and treated him as a beloved son. Another disciple was the tall, handsome and witty Brother Masseo, whose humility Francis put to the test by appointing him cook. Masseo discharged his lowly duties with such good grace and meekness that Francis delighted to have him as his companion. Another stalwart was Brother Giles, who would turn his hand to anything—carrying wood, making baskets, clearing out kitchens, burying the dead. Sometimes he would hire himself out gathering nuts or grapes in return for a portion of the harvest which he would then share with the poor. In his gay acceptance of the hard and simple life, his naïve piety and pithy sayings, Brother Giles seems the very incarnation of the Franciscan spirit.

Francis won two other disciples in Assisi who were to play outstanding parts in his movement. One was Clare, the nineteen-year-old daughter of an ancient and noble family, whose cousin Rufino had also become a companion. In a dramatic midnight elopement Clare left her father's house to join the brothers who were waiting to receive her. There Francis symbolically clothed her with a rough cloak and cut off her hair. She was followed some time later by her sister Agnes, and St Damian's was assigned to them as the first strictly-enclosed home of the 'Poor Ladies'. Clare remained linked in close spiritual friendship to Francis until his death, after which she showed herself a most resolute defender of his ideals when they were threatened with eclipse under the powerful influence of Brother Elias. This controversial personage seems also to have been a native of Assisi and at one time an intimate friend of Francis. A man of superior parts, learned, energetic, austere, a forceful and inflexible administrator, Elias was clearly destined for great things in Church or State. But his spirit seems curiously alien to that of the movement he was in time to dominate with such unhappy results.

By 1210, when Francis had reached the age of twenty-eight and had been leading his life of apostolic poverty for about five years, so many companions had gathered round him that he deemed it necessary to go to Rome to seek the Pope's blessing. He still had no clear idea of where his venture would lead, and no wish at all to found a new Order. All he desired was that the Pope would approve their mutual resolve to live as strictly as possible in accordance with gospel precepts. The head of the Church was Innocent III, mightiest of the Vicars of Christ. He listened, reportedly with an initial scepticism which gradually gave place to a respectful perception of what this young movement might mean for the renewal of the spiritual life of the Church, to the unkempt little man, so humble yet so unshakeably convinced of his mission, candid as a child, unlearned but irresistibly eloquent. Sympathetic but still cautious, Innocent gave the suppliants verbal permission to continue in their chosen way of life, and even to preach penitence to the people, and he appointed a cardinal who would

14

both represent them at his court and keep a watchful eye on their doings.

The brothers roamed two by two throughout the length and breadth of Italy, their rough garb and homely speech at first arousing astonishment and sometimes derision. They called themselves 'Friars Minor', for they considered themselves the least of God's servants. Most were laymen; Francis himself never took priestly orders. The friars worked their way wherever possible, but where no work was to be had, begged their bread for the love of God. Thus, they believed, the disciples had set out at Christ's bidding, taking neither purse nor scrip, 'having nothing, yet possessing all things'. Their poverty soon proved the surest of passports, for the people recognized them as brothers. They preached repentance, as the Pope had said they might, and called on all men to cease their feuds and to live in peace with one another. The response was sometimes sensational. After staying for a time in a shack until turned out by a peasant who wanted it for his donkey, Francis and his closest companions set up their headquarters in a clearing in the woods near Assisi around the chapel of St Mary of the Angels, at the Porziuncula, 'the little portion of land', where the Benedictines who owned it allowed them to stay. Francis was invited to preach in the Cathedral. His passionate appeals resulted in the reconciliation of the two chief warring factions. The signed document pledging an end to the feud is still preserved amongst the city's archives.

Francis loved his native Umbria, with its beautiful

valleys and wooded hills, with all the fervour of his poetic and passionate soul. But his love was not merely that of the local patriot or the romantic nature-lover. It was universal and all-embracing, reaching from our lordly Brother Sun and Sister Moon, which he extolled in his great *Canticle of the Creatures*, to the birds who hushed their song when he spoke and the earth-worm he stooped to remove from the danger of trampling feet. His love was utterly unsentimental, lavished alike on inanimate objects or forces—water, fire, rocks—and living things, for all were equally their maker's gift to man. In every creature, and in the elemental forces of nature itself, he saw the image of the Creator. A lamb spoke to him of the Lamb of God, a tree the Cross of Christ, a rock the Rock of Ages.

Living so close to a nature God-given even in its harshness, his heart was lifted in an endless paean of thanksgiving. Possessing nothing and accounting themselves nothing, the friars discovered joy. Resting beside a limpid spring and spreading the scraps of food he had begged on a stone which served as their table, Francis bade Brother Masseo give thanks for the 'treasure' God had bestowed on them. But the friars were no mere vagabonds enjoying the pleasure of a carefree open-air life. Joy was inseparably linked with suffering. These were the two poles between which the soul enamoured of God constantly moved. Praise for the Father's greatness and goodness melted readily into grief over the Son's suffering. And sharing in that suffering led again to joy, as Francis explained to Brother Leo in his incomparable discourse on the nature of perfect joy. The memory of Christ's passion and the awareness of human misery were always vividly present in his heart and ended by imprinting themselves on his body in the mysterious marks of the stigmata.

Solitude in which to pray and contemplate, and action bringing the fruits of contemplation to others, were thus both equally necessary to Francis. The poet who saluted the glorious sunshine found it quite natural to withdraw for days on end into the darkness of a hermit's cave. At times he was even torn with doubt as to whether to devote himself wholly to the contemplative rather than to the active life. With characteristic humility he turned to those whose spiritual insight he most valued and accepted their counsel that he should resume his apostolate. Francis was too much in tune with the simple folk whom he called upon to repent and live in peace and piety to expect them to become in turn preachers or hermits. Theirs was the daily round and the duty to earn their bread and to care for their families. But in doing so, they could still show the same spirit of Franciscan love and humility which animated the Little Poor Man and his companions. Hence there was born the Third Order (the First being the Friars, the Second the sisters, 'Poor Ladies', or 'Poor Clares') of lay men and women pledged to live out the founder's ideals in the workaday world. It proved an innovation of great importance, spreading spiritual renewal throughout the fabric of the church. Many great figures, including

Dante and Giotto, whose art bears the strong imprint of this inspiration, were proud to belong to it, no less than the many who passed their lives in humble Franciscan anonimity.

Because their sense of human brotherhood was universal and their message addressed to one and all, the friars were from the outset missionaries. Francis sent some to his beloved France, and would eagerly have gone with them had not the cardinal appointed to be the young Order's Protector restrained him. Another group travelled through Spain to Morocco where they quickly met martyrdom. Others suffered nearly the same fate at the hands of the Germans who, being unable to understand their speech, took them for madmen or heretics. Francis burned to carry his message to the Muslims and to imitate Christ's passion by the sacrifice of his own life. He made his way to Syria, where the crusaders were besieging Damietta. Sickened by their licence and brutality and convinced that the gospel of love could not be imposed by the sword, he walked across no-man's-land and was taken into the presence of the Sultan. The latter received him with astonishment but listened courteously to his words. If no miraculous conversion followed, it seemed almost as great a miracle to find a Christian who was so wholly Christ-like.

Francis had longed for martyrdom, and his desire was to be granted in a manner he had not foreseen. In North Africa he contracted an eye disease which grew more and more painful and ended by sending him blind. Still more acute was the pain he felt on returning to Italy and discovering what had been happening there in his absence. With the rapid expansion of the Order, differences had developed between those who remained uncompromisingly committed to its early ideals of absolute poverty and simplicity, and those who argued that what was right for a mere handful of wandering friars was no longer fitting for an Order of its present size. They held in particular that the friars should be better educated and organized, and for this they needed to have houses of their own where they could study. One such college had already been established in the university city of Bologna. Francis, usually so gentle, acted with inexorable severity. The brothers (even those who were sick) were made to evacuate their house at once, and the friar who had been responsible for it was solemnly cursed. Learning begat pride, and possessions, even when held in common, were an unforgivable offence against Lady Poverty. Those who were not prepared to renounce them absolutely had no place in the brotherhood which Francis believed he had received God's command to found.

But the strains within the Order were too great to be resolved by drastic action against a few individuals. Nor was it in Francis's nature to go on imposing discipline in this way. He decided to give up his position as head of the brotherhood. Peter Cataneo was chosen as his Vicar General, and after Peter's death, Brother Elias. Under pressure from the Cardinal Protector, Francis was forced to consent to changes which he saw would modify the spontaneous, informal nature of the original movement and bring it more into line with traditional church usage. Intending friars had first to undergo the customary year's novitiate instead of simply giving away their property and taking to the road. A formal Rule needed to be worked out for the Order. When 5,000 friars gathered at the little church at Porziuncula, in what came to be called the Chapter of the Mats, Francis was happy to see that they were still content with these makeshift shelters and with such food as the peasants voluntarily brought to them. But prudence counselled that taking neither scrip nor purse, nor any thought for the morrow, was no longer a virtue where such numbers were concerned. Yet every concession made to prudence seemed to the founder a betrayal, a fresh torment devised for his protracted martyrdom.

Shortly before his death, Francis composed his *Testament* in a final effort to preserve what he believed to be the God-given purity of the movement he had been led to found. He no longer had the power to command, but he could still speak in the name of the Master who had lived a homeless wanderer and died in the stark poverty of the cross. It is an intensely moving document in which he recalls how, whilst still a sinner, he had heard the call to serve the lepers and to abandon his possessions, how others had come to join him, and how they had lived together in simplicity and poverty according to the teaching of the Gospel and with the blessing of the Pope. He exhorted them to go on living 'like wanderers and strangers', faithful to their vow of poverty, resolutely refusing to own any property, houses or churches of their own, but to remain obedient to the appointed ministers of Holy Church and observing all her doctrines and usages. They were not to seek for themselves any privileges from Rome nor to amend or water down in any way the simple Rule he had given them. Then they would be assured of God's gracious blessing.

After the Rule had been drafted and received the Pope's approval, and the great Chapter of the Mats had dispersed, Francis felt an overwhelming longing to be alone with his God. Making his way to a remote mountain called La Verna, he gave himself up for some three weeks to prayer and meditation in a strict solitude which not even the intimate companions who accompanied him were allowed to disturb. He had striven to conform his life as closely as possible to Christ's, and now he wished to express his love by sharing in the supreme agony of Gethsemane and Calvary. His prayer was answered by a mystical experience which left his hands and side imprinted with wounds resembling those made by the nails and spear that had pierced his crucified Lord. Although Francis never afterwards spoke of them and concealed the sight as best he could from others, his body remained clearly marked with the mystery of the stigmata until his death two years later.

Francis died at the Porziuncula in the autumn of 1226, at the age of forty-four. As he lay mortally sick, he composed his great paean of praise to the Creator and his works—Brother Sun and Sister Moon, fire, water, wind, the earth and all God's creatures. On his death-bed he added a final verse of welcome to Sister Death. He could no longer see the world he was leaving, but he asked his companions to turn him towards Assisi for his blessing. Then they laid him on the bare ground where, after he had blessed each of his companions and caused them to break bread together in symbolic token of unity, he died.

The latent differences amongst the sons of St Francis came to a head after his death. The Order split into two factions. On the one side were the Zealots or Spirituals, clinging tenaciously to the early and uncompromising simplicities and looking to the founder's *Testament* as their gospel; on the other, the Brothers of the Common Observance, who took their stand on the Rule, with such concessions as Francis had been forced to make to ecclesiastical usage and prudence. Amongst the Spirituals were numbered Brothers Bernard, Leo and others of the earliest and closest companions. The Common Observance had the support of Brother Elias, the energetic head of the Order, and the Cardinal Protector, now raised to the papal throne under the name of Gregory IX. The dispute crystallized round the issue of the memorial to be built to the founder's memory. Brother Elias lost no time in laying the foundations of a basilica, whose magnificence was in striking and ironic contrast to the Franciscan simplicity of St Damian's and the Porziuncula. The Spirituals were harried and their protests silenced; a few intransigents were driven into open defiance and branded as heretics.

The saint's deeds and sayings quickly passed into legend. Though an inspired and inspiring preacher, Francis always preferred to teach by example rather than precept. Still less ready had he been to take up the pen. His extant writings comprise only the beautiful *Canticle of the Creatures*, his *Testament*, some prayers, thanksgivings, blessings, fragments of sermons, letters and paraphrases of biblical passages. The Rule which he is thought to have drawn up for the Poor Clares has not survived. Nor have the songs which God's troubadour sang on his wanderings, or the other poems he probably composed. Instead, we have a mass of sayings attributed to him, and stories told about him. The most authentic, and also the most moving in their pristine freshness, are naturally those recorded by the companions who were closest to him. Even when tinged with pious nostalgia or a filial concern to preserve the purity of his teaching, they bear the stamp of an unmistakable authenticity and of a uniquely original personality. The glimpses they give us of this little band of men joined together in common service to Lady Poverty are touched with poetry. It is often a poetry of the absurd, of the sublimely absurd, for the Little Poor Man of Assisi and his friends were not ashamed to be accounted fools for Christ's sake. It is this note of holy quaintness, this proneness to the unexpected which is yet profoundly in keeping with the logic of Franciscan wisdom, that gives the sayings and stories collected in the following pages much of their distinctive charm.

Francis, who distrusted human learning, made no

attempt to systematize and develop his teaching. Indeed, he would have disclaimed any originality at all for what he taught. His first attempt to draw up a Rule for his companions seems to have been little more than a short compilation of biblical texts. His concern was simply to go on saying, and to put into practice, what he held to be the basic but neglected truths of the Gospel. His 'Wisdom' is thus enshrined as much in his actions as in his words, and the expression given to it in the following pages will be largely anecdotal.

Many of these stories and sayings were utilized by Thomas of Celano, a friar who had known Francis himself and was commissioned to write the first life of the saint. Nearly twenty years later he produced a new version of his biography largely designed to tone down his earlier praise of Brother Elias, who had subsequently lost the Pope's favour. The disgrace of this inflexible champion of the Common Observance did little, however, to heal the rift in the Order. It was left to the able and virtuous St Bonaventure to attempt this, though we may find it hard to applaud the methods he employed to this worthy end. It has been said that it takes a saint to write the life of a saint. St Bonaventure, however, set himself the task of completely *re-writing* the saint's life, ironing out the obsessive stress on poverty and the disregard of learning which the Common Observance found it so hard to stomach, even to the extent of omitting any mention of the *Testament* in which Francis had enshrined the essence of his teaching. For good measure, St Bonaventure also decreed that all other accounts of St

Francis's life should be destroyed. The faithful and now aged Brother Leo, however, continued to search his memory for his beloved master's words and deeds and to commit them to writing which he then entrusted for safe keeping to the Poor Clares. These, and other early material, survived St Bonaventure's well-meant censorship to swell the treasure-store of fact, poetry and legend which has been such a priceless part of the Franciscan legacy.

How should we sum up the message which Francis brought to his contemporaries and which those who continued his work and recorded his words have sought to transmit to posterity? Perhaps it is best expressed in the familiar prayer commonly ascribed to him:

Lord, make us the instruments of Thy peace. Where there is hatred, let us sow love, where there is injury pardon, where there is doubt faith, where there is despair hope, where there is darkness light, where there is sadness joy. May we seek not so much to be consoled as to console, not so much to be understood as to understand, not so much to be loved as to love. For it is in giving that we receive, it is in pardoning that we are pardoned, it is in dying that we awake to eternal life.

The invocation has in fact been framed in our own anguished times, though it is most certainly imbued with the authentic spirit of the Little Poor Man of Assisi. If Francis never actually said those words himself, he and his companions lived them out to the full and taught their meaning to the world.

STORIES AND SAYINGS

⋆ I ⋆

ONE DAY when Francis was in his father's shop
selling cloth, a poor man came in and begged for
alms for the love of God. Francis was busy and turned
him away. At that moment, the grace of God touched
him, and he reproached himself for his hard-
heartedness. If the beggar had pleaded in the name of
some great lord or noble, he said to himself, I would
surely have given him what he asked. How much
more willingly should I do so for the sake of the King
of Kings, the Lord of creation? From that day he
resolved never again to refuse anything that might be
asked of him for the love of God.

⋆ II ⋆

WHEN his rich companions noticed that Francis was no
longer so eager to join in their merrymaking, they
made fun of him saying: What is the matter with you?
You must be thinking of settling down with a wife!
Francis, moved by the sight of so many needy folk
around him and by a desire to espouse their poverty,
replied: What you say is quite true! I am thinking of
taking the noblest and fairest bride in the whole world!

⋆ III ⋆

WHILST FRANCIS was praying earnestly at the time of

his conversion, the following guidance came to him: All the things you used to love after the flesh and desired to have you must now hate and despise if you would do My will. If you begin to do this, the things which seemed sweet and delightful before will become bitter and intolerable to you. And those things which you used to shrink from will give you immeasurable sweetness. Rejoicing and encouraged by this promise, Francis chanced to meet a leper. Now he had always felt a great loathing for lepers, but he forced himself to get down from his horse, offered the leper money, and kissed his hand. Then, after the leper had given him the kiss of peace, he remounted and rode away.

★ IV ★

FRANCIS, whilst waiting to discover God's will for his life, went to live in a cave and prayed: Who are you, my dear Lord and God, and who am I, your miserable worm of a servant? My dearest Lord, I want to love you. My Lord and my God, I give you my heart and my body, and would wish, if only I knew how, to do still more for love of you!

★ V ★

FRANCIS was walking by the church of St Damian and felt moved to go in and pray before the crucifix. Then he heard these words spoken: Francis, do you not see that my house is being destroyed? Go, therefore, and repair it. Trembling and astonished, he said: Gladly,

Lord, will I do it. For he took the command to refer to that particular church, which was very old and beginning to tumble down. So Francis found the priest and gave him money to buy oil for the lamp before the crucifix, and he went into the city to beg for alms and for stone with which he then set about repairing the church.

★ VI ★

THE PRIEST of St Damian's, a poor man himself, shared his own food in return for the work Francis was doing. But Francis thought to himself that this was not how a beggar should live. Taking a bowl with him, he went from door to door begging alms for the love of God. When he saw the scraps he had collected, he turned from them at first in disgust, for he was not accustomed to eating such things. But he overcame his repugnance and forced himself to swallow them. Then he found such pleasure in eating that it seemed to him he had never tasted anything so good. And he called the crusts given him in charity 'Angels' bread'.

★ VII ★

AFTER he had finished repairing St Damian's, Francis was attending mass and listening to the priest reading from the Gospels. When he heard how Christ had sent out his disciples to preach and commanded them to take no money, shoes or possessions of any kind with them, he was suddenly filled with joy and certainty. That is what I long with all my might to do too! he exclaimed. And he made himself a rough tunic, fastening it with a cord instead of a girdle, and set off to preach to the people and call on them to repent and to serve God.

* VIII *

A PASSER-BY found Francis outside a chapel weeping and sighing as if in great distress. When asked what was troubling him, Francis replied: I am weeping over the sufferings of my Lord Jesus Christ, and I will not be ashamed to go through the whole world and weep over them.

* IX *

THE BISHOP OF ASSISI summoned Francis and reproached him for selling his father's cloth so as to have money to give to the poor. My Lord, I will gladly give back not only the money which belongs to my father, Francis answered, but my clothes as well. Going into an inner chamber, he took off all his clothes and laying the money on them before the eyes of the bishop, his father and all who were present, he exclaimed: Listen everyone, and understand. Up to now I have called Peter Bernardone my father, but as I am now resolved to serve God, I give him back the money which he is so worried about, as well as the clothes I have been wearing and which are his too. From now on I will say: Our Father, who art in heaven, instead of, my father Peter Bernardone. Then the bishop covered Francis with his own cloak and embraced him.

29

★ X ★

WHEN FRANCIS saw that his father was filled with anger and shame to see him living as a beggar and would heap curses on him wherever he found him, he took a certain poor, despised man to be his companion, saying: Come with me, and I will share with you the alms that shall be given me. And whenever you see my father cursing me, I will say to you: Bless me, father! and you shall make the sign of the cross over me and bless me in his stead. And so, when that poor man blessed him, Francis said to his father: Do you not know that God can provide me with a father to give me his blessing in place of your curses?

★ XI ★

AFTER A TIME people began to be attracted to the humble way of life Francis had chosen to lead, and two men came to him saying that they wanted to become his companions. Tomorrow morning we will go to church, he told them, and there we will learn through the gospels how the Lord instructed his disciples. In their simplicity they were unable to find the verses in the Holy Gospel which deal with renouncing the world, so they devoutly prayed that God would show them his will by the first words they should see on opening the book. Francis knelt before the altar with the Bible, and when he opened it he found the passage: If thou wilt be perfect, go and sell that thou hast and give to the poor, and thou shalt have treasure in heaven. He opened the Bible a second and a third time and read: Take nothing for your journey; and, If any man will come after me, let him deny himself. Francis thanked the Lord for having thus confirmed the resolution he already held in his heart, and he said to his two companions: My Brothers, this is our life and our Rule, and shall be so for all who wish to join our community. Go then, and act according to what you have heard!

BROTHER BERNARD, a rich and noble man of Assisi, was the first to give away all his possessions and join Francis. When a certain priest called Sylvester, from whom Francis had bought some stones for St Damian's, saw that money was being given away, he came to Francis and said: Francis, you did not pay me well for those stones! So Francis went to Brother Bernard and took from him a handful of coins which he gave to the priest, saying: Are you paid in full now? The priest went home joyfully with the money, but soon his heart was filled with remorse, as he thought to himself: Here am I, an old man, still coveting temporal things, whilst this young man despises and abhors them all for the love of God! And he began to do penance and afterwards he too gave away all he possessed and joined Francis in poverty.

ST FRANCIS taught his companions to use the greeting: The Lord give you peace! When you proclaim peace by your words, he told them, you must carry an even greater peace in your hearts. Let no one be provoked to anger by you, or be scandalized, but let your gentleness encourage all men to peace, good will and mutual love. For our calling is to heal the wounded, to tend the maimed and to bring home those who have lost their way. For many who today seem to us children of the Devil will yet become disciples of Christ.

★ XIV ★

ONE DAY the Bishop of Assisi said to St Francis: Your way of life without possessions of any kind seems to me very harsh and difficult. My Lord, Francis answered, If we had possessions we should need arms for their defence. They are the source of quarrels and lawsuits, and are usually a great obstacle to the love of God and one's neighbour. That is why we have no desire for temporal goods.

★ XV ★

FRANCIS and Brother Bernard once came to a certain town, and since they were both very hungry they agreed to part company and meet again after they had each gone in quest of alms. But Brother Bernard grew so ravenous as he went begging that he immediately devoured every crust and scrap given him and so saved nothing. When they met again as arranged, Francis said: Look, Brother, what alms God in his goodness has given me! Now put down on this stone whatever you have collected so that we may

32

eat together in God's name. Then Brother Bernard was greatly perturbed, and throwing himself down at his companion's feet he exclaimed: O my father, let me confess my sin! Alas, I have collected nothing. I was so hungry that I ate up everything that was given me on the spot. When Francis heard this he wept for joy and exclaimed as he embraced Brother Bernard: Indeed, my dearest son, you are far better than I am. You are a perfect follower of the Holy Gospel, for you have laid up no store nor taken any thought for the morrow, but have cast all your care upon God.

★ XVI ★

WHEN FRANCIS went to the villages preaching and calling men to repent, he always carried a broom to sweep out dirty churches, for it grieved him exceedingly to see a church not cared for as he would wish. Once, when he was busy in this way, a rustic of great simplicity, whose name was John, heard of it whilst he was ploughing. He at once went to the church and said: Brother, give me the broom. I want to help you. When he had finished sweeping the floor, he said: Brother, for a long time I have wanted to serve God, but I did not know how I could get to you. Now that God has willed that I should see you, I will do anything you say. St Francis rejoiced, for he felt that a man of such simplicity and candour must make a good friar. Brother, if you wish to share our life and company, you must renounce all you have and give to the poor, according to the teaching of the Holy Gospels,

Francis told him. The man promptly returned to the field and unharnessed his oxen, one of which he led back to Francis, saying: For many years I have served my father and all my family, and I will claim this ox as my portion and give it to the poor as you think best. But when the man's parents and younger brothers, who were still children, saw that he meant to leave them, they all began to weep aloud and to sob and cry most pitifully. Francis was moved by compassion, and said to his parents: This son of yours wants to serve God, and you should rejoice rather than grieve. All our brothers will be your brothers and sons as well. And he let them keep the ox, because they were so poor. John became his constant companion, and as he was so simple-minded, he thought he must copy everything he saw the holy man do. Thus, whenever Francis knelt down or raised his hands to heaven, even when he coughed or sighed, John would do exactly the same. Francis, noticing this, corrected him with gentle merriment for behaving in this simple-minded manner. But John answered: Brother, I promised I would do everything that you do, and so it is right that I should copy you in all things.

∗XVII∗

FRANCIS, who before his conversion had loathed and avoided lepers, took special care of them and he taught his companions to do the same. But one leper was so ill-tempered and abusive that the friars complained that they would no longer tend him. Francis went to

see the leper and greeted him with his usual salutation:
May God give you peace, dear brother!

And what peace, retorted the leper, can I receive
from God, who has taken from me my peace and every
good thing, and has made my body a mass of stench
and corruption?

Francis said to him: Brother, be patient, for God
sends us diseases in this world for the salvation of our
souls. When we endure them patiently they are a
source of great merit to us.

How can I endure patiently the pains which torture
me day and night? answered the leper. And it is not
merely my disease I suffer from, but the friars you told
to wait on me are insufferable, and do not take care
of me as they ought.

Francis perceived that the leper was possessed by the
spirit of evil, and he went away to pray for him. Then,
returning, he said: My son, since you are not satisfied
with the others, I will wait on you myself.

That is all very well, the leper said, but what can
you do for me more than the others?

I will do whatever you wish, replied Francis.

Very well, said the leper. I want you to wash me
from head to foot, for I stink so badly that I am dis-
gusted with myself.

Then Francis quickly heated some water with many
sweet-smelling herbs. Next, he took off the leper's
clothes and began to bath him, whilst another brother
poured the water over him. And, by a divine miracle,
wherever Francis touched him with his hands the
leprosy disappeared and the flesh became perfectly

sound. Then, as the flesh healed, the soul of the wretched man was healed also, and he began to feel a lively contrition for his sins and to weep bitterly for them.

⋆ XVIII ⋆

THREE ROBBERS, notorious for the crimes they had been committing in the district of Monte Casale, came to the friary there and asked Brother Angelo, its guardian, for food. What, you robbers and cruel murderers, have you no shame? Brother Angelo answered them harshly. You not only rob others of the fruit of their labours but now you come impudently scrounging the very alms given to the servants of God! Begone, and never show yourselves here again!

Shortly afterwards Francis returned with a bag full of bread and a flask of wine he and his companions had been given. When the guardian told him how he had chased the robbers away, Francis rebuked him sharply, saying: You have behaved cruelly. Sinners are brought back to God by kindness more than by harsh reproofs. I command you by holy obedience to take at once this bread and wine and seek the robbers over hill and dale until you find them. Then you are to offer it to them from me, kneeling down before them and humbly asking their pardon for your sin of cruelty. Entreat them in my name to do no more ill but to fear God and cease harming their neighbours. And if they will do this, I promise to provide for their needs and see they always have enough to eat and drink. After that, you may humbly return hither.

Brother Angelo did everything that had been commanded him, while Francis prayed God to convert the
robbers. After some time they returned with the
brother, and when Francis gave them the assurance of
God's forgiveness, they entered the Order and began
to live a life of great penance.

* XIX *

FRANCIS used to teach his friars to think no more of
money than they would of dung. One day a layman
happened to enter the church of St Mary of the Angels
to pray, and as an offering for his petition left some
money behind the crucifix. When he had gone, a friar
who was very simple picked the money up and laid
it on the window-sill. When Francis heard of this and
the friar saw himself discovered, he came running to
beg forgiveness and, prostrating himself on the ground,
declared himself ready to be punished. Francis scolded
him severely for having touched the money and
ordered him to take it up from the window-sill and
carry it in his mouth to the dunghill outside and leave
it there.

* XX *

FRANCIS and Brother Masseo arrived very hungry at a
certain town and began, according to their Rule, to
beg their bread for the love of God. Francis went along
one street, and Brother Masseo along another. But as
Francis was small and unimpressive to look at, people
who did not know him took him for a wretched little

fellow and he managed to collect from them only a few scraps. Brother Masseo, however, was a tall man of handsome appearance, and so he was given a good deal—fine large pieces of bread, and even whole loaves. When they had finished begging they met outside the town in a place where there was a beautiful spring beside a fine, broad stone on which each set out the alms they had collected. When Francis saw that the pieces of bread received by Brother Masseo were far better and larger than his own, he was overjoyed and said: Oh Brother Masseo, we are not worthy of such a great treasure! This he repeated several times, and Brother Masseo answered: Dear father, how can there be any talk of treasure where there is such poverty, and such a lack of the things we need? We have no dish, no bowl, no tablecloth, no house, no table, no man or maid to serve us. Then Francis said: That is what I call a great treasure—that there is not a single thing prepared by human hands, but what there is has been provided by divine providence, as we see by the bread we have collected, by this beautiful stone which is our table and by this clear spring. So I pray God to fill our hearts with love for his treasure of Holy Poverty.

* XXI *

FRANCIS said: We have no right to glory in ourselves because of any extraordinary gifts, since these do not belong to us but to God. But we may glory in crosses, afflictions and tribulations, because these are our own.

ONE DAY, when Francis had gone out of his cell, a certain friar went to it and afterwards came to the place where Francis was. Where do you come from, Brother? Francis asked. I have been to your cell, the other answered. Because you have called it mine, Francis said to him, another must use it in future, for I shall not go there again. And he added: When the Lord was in the wilderness fasting forty days and forty nights he did not have a cell or house made for him but stayed amongst the bare rocks.

BROTHER GILES was a simple man who felt no wish to preach. He used to accompany Francis and wait until he had finished preaching, when he would turn to the people and say: What he says is true! Listen to him and do as he says.

ONE DAY Francis was walking along the road with Brother Masseo, who had gone on a little way ahead. When they reached a place where three ways met Brother Masseo asked: Father, which road shall we take? The one God wills us to take, answered Francis. But how are we to know God's will? asked Brother Masseo. By the sign which I will show you, Francis said. At the crossroads where you are now standing, I command you by the merits of holy obedience to turn round and round on the same spot, as children do, and not to stop turning until I tell you.

So Brother Masseo began to turn round and round, and he went on turning for so long that he fell to the ground several times from the giddiness which results from doing this. But as Francis did not bid him stop and he wished to obey him faithfully he got up and went on again. At length, when he was spinning quite fast, Francis cried: Stop! And don't move! So he stopped, and Francis asked him: Which way are you facing? Towards Siena, Brother Masseo replied. That is the way God wishes us to go, said Francis. . . .

Now at that very time certain men of Siena were fighting, and two of them had already been killed. When Francis got there, he spoke to them in such a devout and saintly manner that they were reconciled. When the bishop heard of the holy work that Francis had done, he invited him to his house and entertained him with great honour that day and also that night. The following morning, Francis roused his companion very early and left without the bishop's knowledge.

This led Brother Masseo to murmur as they went their way, saying to himself: What has this good man been up to now? He makes me spin round and round like a child and then he goes off without a word of thanks, or saying anything at all, to the bishop who did him so much honour! And it seemed to Brother Masseo that this conduct was unseemly. But later, after God had enlightened him, he thought better of it and reproached himself, saying in his heart: You are too proud, Brother Masseo, for you pass judgement on the ways of God and deserve hell for your presumptuous pride! Yesterday Brother Francis performed such holy things that they could not have been more wonderful if an angel of God had done them.

Now all the things Brother Masseo was turning over in his heart God revealed to Francis as they walked along. So he called the friar to him and said: Hold fast to those things you have just been thinking, for they are good and profitable and inspired by God; but your earlier objections were blind, vain, proud and sent you by the Devil. Then Brother Masseo clearly perceived that Francis knew the secrets of his heart, and was guided by the divine wisdom in everything he did.

★ XXV ★

FRANCIS was so overflowing with charity that he loved not only his fellow-men, but all his fellow-creatures—birds, beasts, fishes and even creeping things—for in each one of them he perceived the handiwork of his Father, and if he chanced to see anything suffering pain he, too, suffered with it. Now, of all God's beasts of the field, he loved lambs the best, for in them he beheld the likeness of 'the Lamb that was slain'. Once, when he was journeying with Brother Paul, he fell in with a goatherd amongst whose goats he noticed a lamb meekly skipping around and nibbling a little grass. Look at that lamb, he said to Brother Paul, how like it is to Christ amongst the proud Pharisees! Let us, for love of him, purchase it and so deliver the gentle creature from the company of those goats. Brother Paul was much distressed to think that they had no money to offer the man, and nothing other than their poor habits, all patched and ragged. As they were wondering what to do, they were overtaken by a merchant on his way to market. When he learned the cause of their grief, he paid the goatherd his price for it and after they had given thanks to God and to the merchant, they took the lamb and went on their way rejoicing. Presently they came to Osimo, where the bishop was quite taken aback to see the lamb and the friars making much of it, but when Francis had expounded the parable he was touched and gave glory to God for their simplicity. On the morrow, at Brother Paul's suggestion, they sent the lamb to the Poor Ladies, who tended it with loving care. In due time they made a habit out of its wool and sent this to Francis, who received it with much joy and affection.

XXVI

FRANCIS and one of his brothers were once walking through the Venetian marshes where a great number of birds were nesting amongst the rushes and singing. Our sisters the birds are praising their Creator, he said to his companion. Let us go amongst them and chant the Lauds and the canonical hours. The birds did not fly away as they approached but kept up such a twittering that Francis and the friar could not hear each other's responses, so he turned and said to the birds: Sister birds, stop singing until we have finished the praises we owe to the Lord! Thereupon the birds at once fell silent and they kept quiet until Francis and the friar had finished saying the hours and chanting the Lauds. Then Francis gave them leave to sing praises to the Lord after their own fashion, and the birds at once resumed their songs.

* XXVII *

ONE DAY, when the hour for Matins came round, Francis said to Brother Leo: Dearest Brother, we have no breviary from which to say Matins, but so that we may spend our time praising God I will speak and you shall answer as I will teach you. I shall say: O Brother Francis, you have done so much wrong and committed so many sins in this world that you deserve to go to hell. And you, Brother Leo, will answer: That is quite true, and you deserve to go to the very depths of hell.

And Brother Leo, with dove-like simplicity, replied: Willingly, Father; begin then, in God's name.

Then Francis began to say: You have done so much wrong and committed so many sins in this world that you deserve to go to hell. And Brother Leo answered: God will work so much good through you that you will go to Paradise!

That is not what you are to answer, Brother Leo, Francis said. But when I say: O Brother Francis, you have sinned so sorely against God that you deserve to be accursed by him, then you are to reply: Truly you deserve to be numbered amongst the damned. And Brother Leo answered: Willingly, Father.

Then Francis, beating his breast with many sighs

43

and tears, cried out: O my Lord, God of heaven and earth, I have committed so many sins and offences that I fully deserve to be accursed by you. And Brother Leo answered: O Brother Francis, God will perform such things through you that you will be singularly blessed amongst the blessed!

Francis was amazed that Brother Leo kept on answering the opposite of what he had told him and he rebuked him with these words: Why do you not answer as I told you? I command you under holy obedience to answer as I tell you. I shall say: O Brother Francis, you miserable wretch, do you expect God to have mercy on you, seeing that you have committed so many sins against the Father of mercy and the God of comfort that you are unworthy to find mercy? And you, dearest Brother, are to reply: You are assuredly unworthy to find mercy.

But when Francis said: O Brother Francis, miserable wretch . . . and the rest, Brother Leo answered: Our Heavenly Father, whose mercy is infinitely greater than your sins, will show you great mercy, and give you much grace besides!

At this, Francis, mildly angered and perturbed despite his patience, said to Brother Leo: How can you dare to act against holy obedience, and why do you keep on answering the very opposite of what I ordered you?

Brother Leo answered very humbly and respect-fully: God knows, my father, that each time I fully intended to answer as you told me, but God makes me speak as he wills and not as I intended.

Francis was filled with wonder and said to Brother Leo: I entreat you most lovingly to answer me this time as I tell you.

Speak, in God's name, Brother Leo answered, and this time I will most certainly answer as you wish.

And Francis said, with tears: O Brother Francis, miserable wretch, do you imagine that God will have mercy on you?

Brother Leo answered: You will receive great grace from God, and he will exalt and glorify you for ever, for the humble will be exalted! And I cannot speak otherwise, for God is speaking through my lips.

XXVIII

THERE was once a friar who offended against the rule of Obedience. Francis sent for him and rebuked him sternly. Then he ordered the others to take him outside and make him stand in a pit whilst they filled it up with earth. When the man was buried up to his neck Francis called out: Are you dead yet, Brother? Yes, Father, the man humbly replied, or at least I ought to be on account of my sins. Then Francis told the friars to dig him out again, and he said to him: Go now, Brother, and if you are really dead to the world and the flesh as a good friar ought to be dead, then you will obey your superiors in all things and will never be reluctant to do whatever you are told, just as a corpse has to submit to everything.

★XXIX★

WHEN FRANCIS was on a preaching tour with Brother Leo, it happened that his companion began to flag through sheer exhaustion. So as they were passing a vineyard, Francis went in and picked a bunch of grapes which he gave to Leo. But an angry peasant saw what he had done and gave him a good beating. Afterwards, as they went their way, Francis complained of the hard knocks he had received on Brother Leo's account and could not bring himself to give thanks to God for his suffering. Brother Leo has eaten well, but Brother Francis has been well beaten, he said. Brother Leo has had a good meal, but Brother Francis has paid for it with his body.

★XXX★

ONCE, when Brother Peter Cataneo saw that St Mary of the Angels was crowded with visiting friars and that the alms he had would not be enough to provide for them, he said to Francis: Dear Brother, whatever shall I do? Allow us, I pray, to put aside part of the property of the novices who come to join the Order, so as to have something in reserve in times of need. Francis answered: Away with the sort of piety, dearest Brother, which would have us disregard the Rule for the sake of men! Then what am I to do? asked Brother Peter. Strip bare the Blessed Virgin's altar, Francis replied. Take away its various ornaments, if you cannot help the needy in any other way. Believe me, the Holy Mother would far rather have us keep her Son's teaching and strip her altar than see her altar adorned and the Gospel neglected. The Lord will surely send someone to restore those ornaments which he has lent us.

* XXXI *

FRANCIS made friends with a nobleman of Rome called Matteo de' Rossi, who invited him to dinner. Whilst they were waiting for their master to arrive, the servants began to distribute the daily dole to the beggars who gathered at the palace gate. When he realized what was going on, Francis slipped away to join the crowd and was given his share. Matteo came home and the servants started looking for Francis who was nowhere to be found. At last Matteo caught sight of him squatting amongst the poor in the courtyard. The nobleman then hurried out and sat down beside him, saying: Since you won't eat with me, Brother Francis, I must needs eat with you! And he asked Francis to admit him to the Third Order and to teach him its Rule.

* XXXII *

FRANCIS showed great tenderness for all of God's creatures, however humble. Remembering the Psalmist's words: As for me, I am a worm and no man, he would pick up any earth-worms he found in his path and carry them to safety, so that passers-by would not tread them underfoot.

ONCE, in the middle of the night, when the brothers were asleep, one of them suddenly cried out: I am dying! I am dying! They all started up in amazement and terror. Francis had the lamp lit and asked: What ails you, Brother? Why should you be dying? The man answered: I am dying of hunger. At this Francis at once had a meal prepared and with his usual charity and tact he shared it with the brother, so that the latter should not feel ashamed to eat alone, and by his wish all the other friars also ate. After they had finished he said to then: My dear Brothers, I tell you that everyone must consider his own nature. If one of you can sustain himself with less nourishment than another, I would not have one who needs more food imitate him, but I wish him to have regard to his nature and allow his body what it needs, so that it may be in a fit state to serve his spirit. For God will have mercy and not sacrifice.

★XXXIV★

THE FRIARS did not at first think it necessary to make any preparations before setting out on a mission to foreign lands. The first who went to Germany knew nothing of the language except the word *Ja*, so the people could not understand what they said, nor could they understand the people. When someone asked whether they were heretics, the friars answered: *Ja*, *Ja*; so they were beaten and driven away. When Francis called for others to go on a second mission to

Germany, many came forward and offered to do so. A certain friar called Giordano, who was writing a chronicle of the Order, went over to talk to them: Now you are here, you are one of us, the volunteers told him, You must come too. No, I will not! Brother Giordano exclaimed in alarm. I am not one of you, and I don't want to go at all! The Superior asked the chronicler to say whether he would go or not. Brother Giordano, fearing it might be a sin against obedience to refuse, did not know what to say. I do not want to go, he answered, and I do not want not to go. In the end Brother Giordano went with the others, and this time the mission was a success and many were converted.

* XXXV *

ONE DAY, when Francis was coming out of a wood where he had been praying, Brother Masseo went to meet him. Wishing to put his humility to the test, he said to him, affecting a jeering tone: Why *you*? Why *you*?

What do you mean by that? Francis asked him.

I mean, why should it be *you* all the world is running after, and why does everybody want to see you, listen to you and obey you? You are not handsome, nor very learned, nor of noble birth. Why, then, should all the world be running after you?

When Francis heard this, he rejoiced in the spirit and raising his face to heaven, he remained a long time with his mind uplifted to God; after a while, returning to himself, he fell on his knees and gave praise and

49

thanks to God. Then he turned to Brother Masseo in great fervour of spirit and said: You want to know why it should be me the world is running after? This is granted me because the eyes of the most high God, which look upon the good and the evil in every place, could not find among sinners anyone more vile, worthless and sinful than me, or any baser creature on earth for the marvellous work he intends to perform. So he has chosen me to confound the nobility, the greatness, the power, the beauty and the wisdom of the world. He has done this that men may understand that all virtue and all good proceed from him alone, and not from any creature.

XXXVI

FRANCIS once saw in a dream a little black hen with feathered wings and feet like a tame dove, who had so many chicks that she could not shelter them beneath her wings. They kept running round and round the hen without any protection. When he woke up he began to ponder that vision and all at once he knew through the Holy Spirit what it meant. I am that hen, he said, small in stature and black by nature. I must be as simple as a dove; I have wings with which to fly up to heaven. And the Lord of his great mercy has given me many sons whom I cannot defend by my own power. I must therefore commend them to Holy Church, so that she may protect and govern them under the shadow of her wings. So he went to speak to Pope Honorius in Rome to entreat him to make

Cardinal Ugolino of Ostia, who was a good friend of
the Brothers, the Father of the whole Order.

WHEN FRANCIS and Brother Masseo were once on
their way to Rome the bishop of a certain city through
which they had to pass received news of their coming
and, since he had heard them accounted holy, resolved
to do them honour. As soon as Francis learned that the
bishop, wearing his episcopal robes and attended by
his clergy, was approaching he exclaimed: Oh Brother
Masseo, then we are undone! Masseo asked him why.
We are indeed undone! Francis repeated. Don't you
see that all those people are coming out to show us
honour? Whatever are we to do? Pray, Brother
Masseo, that God will deliver us from such a shameful
thing. As the bishop and his clergy drew near, Francis
espied a heap of potter's clay by the roadside. Lifting
up his tunic, he stepped into it and began kneading
the clay with his feet. When the bishop saw Francis
thus engaged he held him in low esteem and turned
back. But on thinking it over later, he began to feel
edified. So when Francis entered the city, the bishop
received him with love and reverence and gladly gave
him leave to preach to the people.

A BOY who had once been sent on an errand to the
friars thought to himself: If I manage to see the blessed

Francis and to speak with him, then I shall know I am saved. But if I am turned away, then I shall know I am damned. So when he came to the friars, he asked if he might see Francis. But Brother Angelo would not let him. My dear son, he said to him, Brother Francis is praying, and he has strictly commanded us not to disturb him except in great necessity. When the boy heard this, he threw himself on the ground in tears, persuaded that he was damned. Then he opened his heart to Brother Angelo who took him by the hand and led him to the place where Francis was. When Francis saw them, he cried out very excitedly: What's the matter, Brother Angelo? What's the matter? Brother Angelo calmed Francis and explained why they had come. Then Francis embraced the boy and comforted him, putting his own girdle round him. My dear son, he said, Take care never to allow such thoughts to enter your head again, for you must know that they are very dangerous.

* XXXIX *

WHEN FRANCIS was returning from Siena he met a poor man and said to his companion: Brother, we must give this cloak back to the poor man to whom it belongs, for we have borrowed it until we should happen to meet someone poorer than ourselves. His companion, aware of the Father's necessity and fearing that he might provide for another at the cost of neglecting himself, tried to dissuade him. But Francis handed over the cloak, saying: I will not be a thief; it

would be counted to us as theft if we did not give to
one in greater need.

FRANCIS was once told that at Paris the brothers had
chosen as their Master a learned Professor of Theology
who greatly edified both clergy and laity. I am afraid,
he said with a sigh, that such men will end by killing
my little plant. The true Masters are those who set an
example to their neighbours in good works and kindness. For a man is learned in so far as he works for
others; he is wise in so far as he loves God and his
neighbours; and he is good preacher in so far as he
knows how to do good works faithfully and humbly.

THOUGH FRANCIS dearly loved Clare, Agnes and all
her companions at St Damian's, he saw that it was not
wise for the friars to associate too closely with them.
He even did not wish them to be referred to as 'sisters'.
The Lord has delivered us from wives, he said, and
now the Devil wants us to have sisters. So he wished
them to be known rather as 'Poor Ladies'.

FRANCIS wrote to a Superior exhorting him to treat
offenders with compassion: You should not let a
single brother in the world, whatever sin he may have

53

committed, come before your eyes and depart without having found mercy with you. And should he not ask mercy of you, then you must ask it of him. And were he to come before you a thousand times, love him more than you love me, so as to lead him back on to the right path, and always have compassion on all who sin.

* XLIII *

ONE WINTER'S DAY, when Francis was going from Perugia to St Mary of the Angels, and shivering with cold, he called out to Brother Leo who was walking a few paces ahead: Brother Leo, though God is pleased that the Friars Minor should everywhere be setting a high example of holiness and edification, you must nevertheless write down and diligently note that this is not the source of perfect joy!

Going on a little further, Francis called out a second time: Brother Leo, even though a Friar Minor may give sight to the blind, make the crooked straight, cast out devils, cause the deaf to hear, the lame to walk and the dumb to speak, and even raise the dead to life, write that this is not the source of perfect joy!

And when they had gone a little further, Francis again called out loudly: Brother Leo, even if a Friar Minor knew every language, every science and all scripture, and could prophesy and reveal not only the future but the secrets of the conscience and the soul, note that this is not the source of perfect joy!

Walking on a little further still, Francis again called out loudly: O Brother Leo, even if a Friar Minor could

54

speak with the tongue of angels, tell the course of the stars and the virtues of every herb, even if all the treasures of the earth were revealed to him and he knew the properties of the birds, fishes and all the animals, of men, trees, stones, roots and water—write down that this is not the source of perfect joy!

And after a little while more, Francis called out loudly: O Brother Leo, even if a Friar Minor could preach with such eloquence that he could convert all unbelievers to the faith of Christ, write down that this is not the source of perfect joy!

Francis continued to discourse in this way for the best part of two miles until Brother Leo asked him in great bewilderment: Father, I beg you for God's sake to tell me the source of perfect joy!

And Francis answered him: When we reach St Mary of the Angels, drenched with rain, numb with cold, covered with mud and exhausted by hunger, and we knock at the gate and the porter angrily asks: Who are you? and we answer: Two of your brothers; and he says: You are lying! You are a couple of rascals who go about taking folk in and robbing the poor of alms—be off with you; and if he refuses to open and leaves us standing outside until nightfall in the snow and rain, hungry and frozen; and if we put up with such abuse and ill-treatment patiently and calmly, without complaining, thinking with humility and charity that this porter recognizes us for what we are, and that God moves him to treat us like this—then, Brother Leo, write down that here is the source of perfect joy.

And if we keep on knocking and he comes out in a rage and drives us away like importunate rogues with insults and blows saying: Begone, you worthless thieves; go to the poor-house, for there is no food or lodging for you here; and if we bear this patiently, gladly and charitably, Brother Leo, then write down that here is the source of perfect joy.

And if, driven by hunger, cold and darkness, we persist in knocking and imploring him with tears to open and let us in for the love of God, and he becomes still more furious and says: These are importunate scoundrels, and I will give them what they deserve! and rushes out with a knotted stick, grabs us by the cowl, hurls us to the ground and rolls us in the snow, and trounces us with every knot on his stick; and if we endure this patiently and cheerfully, remembering Our Blessed Lord's sufferings and how we must bear this for love of him—then write down, Brother Leo, that here is the source of perfect joy.

* XLIV *

A VERY LEARNED MAN once wanted to join the Order. When Francis asked the brothers for their opinion, they replied that they thought he would not make a good friar. Then one of them said: Father, do you know what I propose? That we should accept this man if he is willing to cook for us, but not otherwise. The learned man was quite astonished at this proposal, but after considering the matter he told Francis that he was willing to be their cook. So Francis made him serve for a month in the kitchen, and when he saw how humbly he went about his duties, he ordered him to assume the office of Guardian and to preach.

WHEN the time came for the friars' General Chapter, which they held every year at St Mary of the Angels, the people of Assisi, seeing how the brothers were growing in numbers and that there was no shelter other than a small thatched hut of wattle and mud, decided to build a large house of stone and mortar for them. This they did in a few days, with great speed and devotion, without the consent of Francis who was away at the time. When Francis returned to attend the Chapter he was surprised to see the newly-built house. Fearing that this might encourage the friars to have similar large houses built for them elsewhere, and wishing the place to remain a pattern and example for all the other hermitages of the Order, he climbed up onto the roof, before the Chapter ended, and called the friars up too. With their help he then started to throw down the tiles with which the house was roofed, intending to demolish it to the foundations. Some knights of Assisi, who were there guarding the place on account of the great crowds of onlookers, saw that Francis and the other friars meant to destroy the house and at once called out to him: Brother, this house belongs to the municipality of Assisi, on whose behalf we are here. So we forbid you to destroy our house. When Francis heard this, he said to them: Well, if this

house is yours, I will not touch it. And he and the
other friars at once came down.

⋆ XLVI ⋆

FRANCIS used to tell the friar who chopped wood for
the fires never to fell the whole of a tree, but to cut it
in such a manner that part should remain whole, out
of love for him who was crucified on the tree of the
cross for our salvation. He likewise told the friar who
tended the garden not to use all the ground merely for
planting edible herbs, but to leave a plot for plants
that in time would bear our sisters the flowers, out of
love for him who is called 'the rose of Sharon and the
lily of the valley'. He always wanted the brother
gardener to keep part of the garden for flowerbeds,
sowing and planting there all fragrant herbs and all
plants that produce beautiful flowers, so that in their
season all men should be moved to praise God by the
sight of these herbs and blossoms.

⋆ XLVII ⋆

FRANCIS came with a number of missionary friars to
Ancona where they hoped to take ship to the Holy
Land. Finding difficulty in securing a passage for so
many, he said to them: The owners of the ship refuse
to take us all. I have not the courage to choose which
of you should accompany me and which stay behind,
as you might think I do not love you all alike. So let
us try to learn God's will. Then he called a child who

was playing near by and got him to point with his finger to the eleven friars who were to set sail.

FRANCIS wished to do honour to the Virtues by composing the following song: Hail, Queen Wisdom, God save thee with thy holy sister pure Simplicity! Hail, Lady holy Poverty, God save thee with thy holy sister Humility! Hail, Lady holy Charity, God save thee with thy sister, holy Obedience! Hail, all you holy virtues, may God save you—he from whom you come and have your being. There is not a man in the world who could possess even one of you unless he has first died [to himself]. He who possesses one and does not offend the others, possesses them all; but he who violates even one, possesses none at all and violates them all.

ONCE when Francis was passing near a certain village he noticed a large flock of birds of different kinds all gathered together. Leaving his companions and going eagerly towards them, as they seemed to be awaiting him, he gave them his accustomed greeting. Surprised that they did not fly away as they generally do, he started talking to them: Brother birds, you ought to praise and love your Creator very much! He has given you feathers for clothing, wings for flying, and everything you need. He has made you the noblest of his creatures, for he has appointed the pure air for your habitation. You have neither to sow nor to reap, yet he takes care of you, watches over you and guides you. At this [as he used to relate himself] the birds began to rejoice after their fashion, stretching out their necks, spreading their wings, opening their beaks and looking at him, whilst he went to and fro amongst them, stroking their heads and bodies with the fringe of his tunic, and finally making the sign of the cross over them and sending them away with his blessing.

★ L ★

SOME TIME after preaching to the birds, Francis was walking along with Brother Masseo when he saw another flock not far away. Thinking he would speak to them as he had to the others, he went towards them, but they all flew off at his approach. Then Francis turned back and began to reproach himself bitterly, saying: How presumptuous you have become, you impudent son of Peter Bernardone! You seem to expect God's creatures to obey you just as if you, and not he, were their creator!

★ LI ★

FRANCIS once asked a bishop for permission to preach in his diocese. I am in no need of anyone to help me in my task, the bishop coldly replied. Francis humbly withdrew, but in less than an hour he was back again. What is it, brother, you require of me this time? asked the bishop in surprise. My Lord, Francis said to him,

When a father drives his son out of the door he returns
by the window. Disarmed by such pious persistence
the bishop relented and gave him leave to preach.

A CERTAIN ENGLISHMAN, a doctor of divinity, was once
preaching at the convent of St Damian in the presence
of St Clare and Brother Giles. He had not got far in
his sermon before Brother Giles interrupted him by
crying out: Hold your peace, Master, hold your peace!
I want to preach! The other at once fell silent, and
Brother Giles, with great fervour, uttered words of
God sweet as honey. After a while he said: Now,
Brother, finish the sermon you have begun. At this,
St Clare rejoiced greatly in spirit, saying: Today the
desire of our father Francis has been fulfilled, for he
once said to me: I long for my brothers the clergy to
attain to such humility that a doctor of divinity would
break off his sermon to let a layman preach. I tell you,
my brothers, that this doctor has edified me more than
if I had seen him raising the dead to life.

BROTHER ANGELO was much afraid of evil spirits and
asked Francis to let a brother sleep in his cell and keep
him company at night. Francis said to him: Why fear
weak and feeble foes whose strength, as you well
know, is under God's control? And so that you may
prove this yourself, I command you to go tonight

alone to the top of yonder mountain and cry out in a loud voice: Come on now, you proud devils, do your utmost and vent your fury on me! The friar humbly did as he was told, and no devil came near him; so from then on he lost all fear of them.

★ LIV ★

A DOCTOR OF THEOLOGY once questioned Francis about the words of Ezekiel: If thou speakest not to warn the wicked from his evil way, his soul will I require from thine hand. There are many, good father, whom I know to be in mortal sin, he said, but whom I do not warn from their evil way; will then their souls be required from my hands? Francis answered that he was only an ignorant man and that others could expound the scriptures better. But when the doctor pressed him he replied: I understand it thus: that the servant of God must so glow and shine by his own saintly life that the light of his example and his holy conversation should be a rebuke to all the ungodly. In this way, I say, the splendour of his life and the sweet odour of his good repute will warn all wicked men from their evil way.

★ LV ★

THE FRIARS often heard Francis say: If I could speak to the Emperor I would beg and persuade him, for the love of God and for my sake, to make a special law forbidding anybody to catch our sisters the larks and kill them, or harm them in any way. Likewise all civic authorities and the lords of castles and villages should be asked every year, on Christmas Day, to compel the people to scatter corn and other grains on the roads outside the towns and castles, so that our sisters the larks and other birds should have enough to eat on that most solemn feast-day; and that out of reverence for the Son of God, who on that night was laid in the manger by the Blessed Virgin Mary between an ox and an ass, whoever owns an ox and ass should give them a good feed on that night.

THE FRIARS once complained to Francis: Can you not see that the bishops often do not let us preach, and we are frequently made to wait for days on end before we are allowed to proclaim the word of God? It would be best to obtain from the Pope a privilege to allow us to preach. It would be for the good of souls. Francis answered them: I would rather see the prelates first converted by humility and respect. For when they have seen us humble and respectful towards them, they themselves will beg us to preach and convert the people. As for me, I ask of God no privilege except that of having none, and to be full of respect for all men, and to convert them, as our Pule ordains, more by our example than by our words.

A POOR OLD WOMAN who had two sons in the Order

once came to the hermitage to beg alms. Have we not something here we can give our mother? they asked Brother Peter Cataneo. (For he used to say that the mother of any friar was his own mother and the mother of all the others.) Brother Peter answered: There is nothing in the house that we could give her, for she needs something with which to nourish her body. In the church we have only one New Testament from which we read the lessons at Matins. Francis said: Give our mother the New Testament so that she can sell it for her needs. Noticing the friar's surprise, he added: Has she not given our Order her two sons?

★ LVIII ★

BROTHER JUNIPER was so moved by compassion for the poor that if ever he met anyone who seemed more poorly clad than himself he would at once cut off a sleeve, or a cowl, or some piece of his tunic, and give it to the poor man. So the Guardian forbade him to give away his tunic or any part of it. One day, meeting a poor man, almost naked, who begged alms of him, he said: I have nothing to give you but my tunic, which I am forbidden by my superior to give. But if you will strip it off me I will not resist. So the poor man stripped him, took the tunic, and left Brother Juniper naked.

★ LIX ★

IN ORDER to discourage those who were always wanting to be gadding about on pilgrimages, Brother

Masseo used to say: It is better to go to the living saints than to the dead saints; that is to say, to good men who are alive, rather than to visit the tombs of the saints. For the living saints will teach you of the dangers they have passed through, and the temptations of the spirit and of the flesh that they have overcome.

⋆ LX ⋆

FRANCIS was once returning with Brother Leo from Siena with a heavy heart, because they had been ill-received there. He was also anxious lest St Clare, whom he had left in Assisi, should weaken in her resolve to lead a life of great mortification. When they came to a well he felt he could go no further, and stood gazing down into the still water. Suddenly he raised his head and exclaimed joyfully: Brother Leo, my dearest son, what do you think I have seen in the water of the well? The reflection of the moon, Father, replied Brother Leo. No, Brother Leo, I did not see Sister Moon, said Francis. But through the mercy of God I have seen the true face of our sister Clare, and it was so pure and full of holy joy that my fears have vanished. I know now that our sister partakes of the holy joy which God gives to his dear ones by pouring on them the blessings of holy poverty.

⋆ LXI ⋆

ABOVE all inanimate creatures Francis loved the sun and fire with most devotion, for he used to say: In the morning when the sun rises everyone ought to praise God who created him for our good, for by him our eyes are enlightened by day; and in the evening, when night comes on, everyone ought to give praise for Brother Fire, because by him our eyes are enlightened at night. For we are all as it were blind, but the Lord by these two brothers enlightens our eyes, and therefore we ought specially to praise the Creator for these and other creatures which we daily use. Which thing he himself always did, down to the day of his death.

✶ LXII ✶

THE BROTHERS had a steward who was often murmuring about others and telling tales of the bad things he had seen them do or heard reported of them. Brother Masseo was distressed at this and at last took the man aside and said to him: My son, set before you, I pray, the good deeds of good men and of the saints; in this way, from bad you will become good, and from good better. But if you keep before your eyes the deeds of bad men, thinking about them and telling others of them, from good you will become bad, and from bad worse.

✶ LXIII ✶

ST ANTONY OF PADUA often preached boldly against the cruelties of the tyrant Ezzelino of Romano, and the latter, artfully wishing to test his virtue, sent him a splendid present by the hand of his servants, whom he charged, saying: Present this humbly and devoutly to Brother Antony from me. If he takes it, kill him on the spot; if he indignantly refuses it, come back and do him no harm. They came before him and said: Your son Ezzelino commends himself to your prayers and begs you to accept this little gift, which he sends out of devotion to you. But St Antony, with great indignation reviled them and refused it all, saying that he would take nothing that was plundered from men, that all their stuff might go to perdition, and that they were to go away at once lest the place should be defiled by their presence. When they reported to the tyrant everything that had happened he said: He is a man of God. Let him alone; he may say whatever he likes in future.

LXIV

SEEING one of his companions walking along with bent head and gloomy countenance, Francis rebuked him, saying: Even though you are sorry for your sins, Brother why do you make outward show of grief for your wrong-doings? Keep this sorrow between yourself and God, and pray that in his mercy he may forgive you and restore to your soul the joy of his healing, of which it has been deprived by sin. But in front of me and others show yourself as always having joy; for it is not fitting for a servant of God to show sadness outwardly, or to have a clouded face.

LXV

FRANCIS taught: Brother Body must be provided for

with discretion, dearest Brothers, lest the tempest of sloth be raised in him. For the servant of God should satisfy his body with discretion as regards food, drink, sleep and its other needs, so that he may not be wearied with vigils and reverent persistence in prayer, and that Brother Body may not be able to complain. But if Brother Body, after eating enough food, should then grumble and be negligent, slothful, or sleepy in prayers, vigils, and other good works, let him know that a lazy beast needs the spur, and an ass that will not move requires the goad. Then let him be chastised for a bad and lazy beast who wants to eat but not to earn his keep or carry his load.

✴ LXVI ✴

SEEING Brother Masseo, who was naturally of a cheerful countenance, looking sad, his companions asked him the reason. I am sad, he replied, because I cannot get to the point of feeling that if anyone cut off my hands or feet, or plucked out my eyes, though I had served him to the best of my power, I could still not love him as much as I did before, or be equally pleased to hear men speak well of him.

✴ LXVII ✴

FRANCIS once met a poor man whom he had known in former days and said to him: Brother, how are you? The other began angrily to heap curses on his lord, who had taken away all his goods, saying: I am but in a sorry way, thanks to my lord—God Almighty curse him! Francis, pitying him in soul more than in body, because he was persisting in mortal hatred, said to him: Brother, forgive your lord for the love of God, that you may deliver your soul, and it may be that he will restore what he has taken from you. Otherwise, having lost your property, you will lose your soul as well. I cannot forgive him from my heart, said the man, unless he first restores what he has taken away. Then Francis, having a cloak on his back, said: Look, I give you this mantle, and I entreat you for the love of the Lord God to forgive your lord. The man's heart was forthwith softened by this act of kindness, and he took the gift and forgave the wrongs he had suffered.

* LXVIII *

WHEREVER Francis found any writing, either sacred or secular, whether by the way, in a house, or on the floor, he picked it up most reverently and placed it somewhere safe in case it contained the name of the Lord or something connected with it. One day, when one of the Brothers asked him why he so diligently picked up even writings of pagans, and writings which made no mention of the name of the Lord, he gave this answer: My son, it is because the letters are there of which the most glorious name of the Lord God is composed. The good that is in the writing belongs, moreover, not to the pagans nor to any men, but to God alone, from whom all good comes.

LXIX

Two Friars Minor once complained to Brother Giles that they had been unjustly driven out of their own land by the Emperor Frederick, the persecutor of the Church. Surely you cannot be true Friars Minor! Brother Giles exclaimed. You ought to pity Frederick, as the greatest of sinners, and pray for him, that the Lord would soften his heart, and not to murmur against him for driving you out of your own land. If you are truly Friars Minor, you can have no land of your own.

LXX

Wishing to test the suitability of two young men who wanted to join his Order, Francis asked them to come with him into the garden, saying: Come with me and plant cabbages for the friars' food, just as you see me do. So he took the plants and put them in the earth upside down, with the roots above and the leaves under the ground. One of the young men, who was truly obedient, kept exactly to this way of planting, but the other, with a smattering of human wisdom, disapproved of this method as being unusual with gardeners, and declared that cabbages should be planted the other way round. Then Francis said to him: Son, imitate me, and do just as I do. But the other refused, thinking that what they were doing was foolish. Then the man of God said: Brother, I see that you are a great master. Go your way. For a simple and humble Order does not need such masters, but rather

70

simple and foolish persons, like this companion of yours.

BEFORE sending them out on a mission, Francis addressed his friars in these words: Even though you are on a journey, your conversation must be as humble and honest as though you were in a hermitage or your cell. For wherever we are and walk, our cell is always round us, because Brother Body is our cell, and the soul is the hermit dwelling therein, praying to God and meditating on him.

ONE NIGHT, when Francis was suffering grievous temptations, he took a knotted cord and began scourging himself, saying: See here, Brother Ass! This is how I would treat you! You must feel the whip! But as his temptations did not lessen, he cast off his clothes and went out and threw himself into the deep snow in the garden. Then he took up handfuls of snow and made seven large snowballs, shaping them like columns, which he set upright, as he addressed his body: Look there, this large one is your wife, the next four are your sons and daughters, and the last two your man-servant and your maid-servant, whom you have to wait on you. Now hurry, clothe them quickly, or they will die of cold! But if you find it a burden to have so many responsibilities, then serve God alone! At this the Devil departed in confusion and Francis went back to his cell and praised God.

A CARDINAL tried to persuade Francis to choose for the use of his companions one of the Rules followed by the Orders which already existed in the Church. God has called me by the way of simplicity and humility, Francis answered, and this is the way he wants me and my companions to follow. So I do not wish you to mention to me any other Rule—neither that of St Benedict, nor St Augustine, nor St Bernard, nor any way of life other than this way which has been shown and given me by God's mercy. The Lord said to me that he desired me to be a new sort of simpleton in this world, and that he would lead me by no other way than by that wisdom.

WHEN he went with the Crusaders to Egypt, Francis had an audience with the Sultan whom he hoped to convert. It is said that the Sultan received him standing on a carpet which had a pattern of crosses and started to make fun of him. I see you don't mind trampling on the cross! he scoffed. You should know that there were many crosses on Calvary, Francis answered: The cross of Christ and the crosses of the thieves. We venerate Christ's cross, but you may do what you like with the others. If you want to cover the ground with them, why should we object to walking on them?

FRANCIS was once the guest of a cardinal and asked if

he might stay in an old tower in his garden. But that night he could not sleep at all, and in the morning he said to his companion: Why have the Devils been tormenting us so here? God must have allowed it because my body has been receiving the lord cardinal's hospitality whilst my brothers dwell in hermitages and wretched huts and go through the world suffering hunger and tribulation! So he related to the cardinal what had happened and took leave of him saying: People think me a holy man, but see how easily a few devils can throw me out of a tower!

LXXVI

A CARDINAL, seeing what virtuous lives the friars led, thought it would be of benefit to the Church if some of them were made bishops. But Francis answered him: We have been called Friars Minor and may not presume to become of more account. If you wish us to bear fruit in God's Church, keep us rather in this state to which we have been called, and even force us back to lowliness against our will.

LXXVII

FRANCIS was assailed by doubts as to whether God wished him to spend his life preaching or in solitary prayer. Tell me what you think, he asked his brothers, for I am in great perplexity. I am simple and unversed in speaking, and I feel I have been called to prayer rather than preaching. In prayer we acquire grace and spiritual profit; in preaching, we pass on to others the gifts we have received from heaven. In prayer we gain virtue and attain union with the highest good; in preaching we may meet with distractions and our spirit flags. In prayer we speak with God and he speaks to us, we live with angels and speak with them too; when preaching we place ourselves on a level with men, live amongst them, and we must think, see, say and hear everything that pertains to men. But first and foremost we have to imitate Christ, who came down from heaven to live among men and preach salvation to them. So it seems to me that it may be more acceptable to God to give myself to labouring amongst men rather than withdraw to commune with God. For a long time Francis discussed these things with his friars, but they could reach no conclusion. So he told Brother Masseo to go to St Clare, and also to Brother Sylvester, who was a priest much given to contemplation, and ask them to pray about it and then tell him what they thought. After a time, Brother Masseo returned and was received like a great ambassador by Francis, who knelt before him to hear what St Clare and Brother Sylvester had said. Brother Masseo told them that both were of the opinion that his true vocation was to go on preaching the gospel and to work for the good of souls. Francis humbly listened to their message and, his mind now at rest, did what they advised.

* LXXVIII *

THERE WAS ONCE a friar who had a great appetite for

food but did no work. Francis dismissed him from their company with these words: Go away, Brother Fly, for you are always feeding on your brothers' sweat but remain idle in God's work. You are a Brother Drone who will not share in the toil of the bees but expects to be the first to eat their honey.

LXXIX

FRANCIS said: Know, dear brothers, that courtesy is one of the attributes of God, who courteously makes a present to us of his sun and his rain, giving them both to the just and the unjust. Courtesy is sister to Charity, which causes hatred to vanish and keeps love alive.

LXXX

FRANCIS was once obliged on account of his infirmities to make a journey on horseback. Although it was raining heavily and he was soaked through, he dismounted in order to say his hours, and stood there in the road praying, with the rain beating down on him, as fervently and devoutly as if he were in church or in his own cell. If the body can eat in peace and quietness, although it will assuredly become food for the worms, he said to his companion, with how much greater peace and quietness, devotion and reverence must the soul take its nourishment, which is God himself!

LXXXI

THE CARDINAL who had been the Protector of the

Friars Minor was in time made Pope. One Maundy Thursday, as he had a great love and reverence for them, he donned the Franciscan habit, cord and sandals and went out like them to wash the feet of the poor. It is related that one poor man, not knowing who he was, drove him away saying: You don't know how to wash feet! Go away and send some of the other brothers who can make a better job of it! And the Holy Father got up and mildly obeyed.

★LXXXII★

A CERTAIN ABBOT from Perugia happened to meet Francis on the high road. The abbot dismounted and greeted him reverently, and they spoke together for some time of holy things. When they parted, the abbot asked him to remember him in his prayers. I will do so very willingly, Francis replied. Soon afterwards, Francis said to his companion: Wait here a little for me, Brother, for I must keep my promise. Whilst he was thus praying, the abbot felt such an unwonted warmth and sweetness come over him that his very soul seemed to be melted into God. This transport lasted only a short time, but when he came to himself the abbot knew that what he had experienced was the virtue of the saint's prayer.

★LXXXIII★

FRANCIS said: Charlemagne, Roland, Oliver and the other knights fought against the pagans and conquered

them with much labour and sweat, many falling as
martyrs for the faith. But nowadays there are many
who want to win fame and glory merely by relating
what these saints have done. When news was brought
of the death of the friars who had gone to preach to
the Muslims in Morocco, Francis saluted them as
martyrs but did not wish the brothers to read accounts
of their sufferings. Let each exult in his own martyrdom, he said, and not in that of others.

★ LXXXIV ★

ONE NIGHT Francis was in great pain on account of his
throat, and Brother Juniper prepared some gruel
which he thought would sooth it. Your throat has
grown sore because you are always scolding me!
Brother Juniper said. Francis told him not to be foolish
and refused to touch the gruel. Well then, Father,
Brother Juniper replied, If you will not eat it yourself,
please hold up the candle for me so that I may enjoy it.
Then Francis, who loved Brother Juniper for his
simplicity, saw that they might as well enjoy it
together, and they both drew more nourishment from
this companionship than from the food itself.

★ LXXXV ★

BROTHER JUNIPER was vexed to learn that some people
had heard so much about him that they wanted to
meet him out of sheer curiosity. Seeing some boys
playing see-saw by the roadside, he joined in and

waited for the visitors to arrive. When they came, they were very surprised to see him engaged in this way and expected that he would break off and greet them. But Brother Juniper went on see-sawing harder than ever and paid no attention to them at all. As soon as he saw that they had grown tired of waiting and gone away, he got off the see-saw and went off himself.

* LXXXVI *

FRANCIS feared that learning would make his friars proud and they would then lose their humility and love of poverty. Just suppose, he said, you had subtlety and learning enough to know all things, that you were familiar with all languages, the courses of the stars, and everything else—what is there in that to be proud of? A single demon knows more on those subjects than all the men in this world put together. But there is one thing that the demon can never learn, and which is the chief glory of man: to be faithful to God.

* LXXXVII *

A FEW YEARS after his conversion, in order the better to observe the virtue of true humility, Francis laid down the office of superior before all the brethren assembled in Chapter, saying: From now on I am dead for you. Here is Brother Peter Cataneo, whom I and all of you will obey. And prostrating himself before him, Francis promised him obedience and reverence.

St CLARE and her companions were once eagerly
waiting to see Francis and to hear him preach. After
he had knelt down and prayed, he ordered some ashes
to be brought, and with some of them he traced a circle
about him and the rest he sprinkled on his head. The
Poor Ladies, who had expected a sermon, were amazed
that he should remain kneeling in the midst of the
ashes. All at once Francis got up and in a loud voice
recited the *Miserere*, after which he forthwith departed.
The Ladies began to weep, for they knew what he
wished to teach them; to esteem themselves what they
were in his own eyes—just ashes. And he desired all his
brothers to follow his example; that whilst serving
Christ's handmaids for love of him, they should be like
birds who are always on their guard against the snares
of the fowler.

BROTHER GILES once said to St Bonaventure: Alas,
what shall we simple and ignorant men do to merit
God's favour? My Brother, his Superior replied, you
very well know that it is enough to love the Lord. Are
you very certain of that? Brother Giles asked. Do you
believe that a poor simple woman might please him
as much as a master of theology? The saint assured
him that this was so. On hearing this, Brother Giles
ran out into the street and hailing the first beggar-
woman he met, exclaimed: Rejoice, you poor old
creature, for if you love God you may have a higher

place in the kingdom of heaven than Brother
Bonaventure!

⋆ X C ⋆

A PEASANT whom Francis once met on his travels asked
him: Is it true that you are Brother Francis of Assisi?
On being told that this was so, he went on: Then try
always to be as good as folk say you are, that they may
not be disappointed in their expectations. Francis
immediately got down from the ass he was riding and
prostrating himself before the peasant, thanked him
for his advice.

⋆ X C I ⋆

A CERTAIN NOBLEMAN once asked Brother Giles why
John the Baptist, who was holy from birth, went into
the wilderness to practise penance. Tell me, answered
Brother Giles, why fresh meat is salted when it is still
good? The better to keep it, replied the other. Then the
friar said: Even so was St John seasoned with the salt of
penance that his holiness might be the longer
preserved.

⋆ X C I I ⋆

BROTHER GILES said: If anyone should praise you,
speaking well of you, return the praise to God alone.
If anyone speaks ill of you, or reviles you, cap what he
says by speaking ill—and even worse—of yourself. If
you would make a good case for yourself, try to make
it sound bad, and make out a good case for your

80

companion, putting the blame on yourself and constantly praising—or at least excusing—your neighbour. If anyone picks a quarrel with you and takes you to court, and you want to win the case, then lose it, and you will be the gainer; for if you would go to court in the hope of winning you will find, just when you thought you had gained it, that you were really the loser. So believe me, in all truth, my brother, that the straight way of salvation is the way of loss.

* XCIII *

TWO BROTHERS of the Order of Preachers once came to visit Brother Giles, and as they were talking together about God, one of them said: Reverend Father, St John the Evangelist has spoken things exceeding high and deep about God. Dearest Brother, said Giles, St John tells us nothing about God. Take care, dearest Father, said the other, what is this you are saying? I repeat, said Giles, that St John tells us nothing about God. The Preachers withdrew, scandalized, but Brother John called them back, and pointed to the mountain above the monastery saying: Imagine a mountain of millet seed as big as that, and at the foot a sparrow to eat of it. By how much would the sparrow lessen it in a day, a month, or a year, or how much would it take in a hundred years? It would hardly lessen it in a thousand years, answered the Preachers. Then, said Brother Giles, so boundless is the everlasting Godhead, and so great a mountain, that St John, who was as a sparrow, tells us nothing in respect of his greatness.

81

BROTHER GILES once said: A certain man had neither eyes, hands nor feet. Someone asked him: If anyone gave you back your feet, what would you give him? A hundred pounds, he answered. And if anyone gave you back your hands? All my goods, was his reply. And if anyone gave you light? I would serve him all the days of my life. Then Brother Giles said: Well, my dear brother, the Lord has given you hands, eyes and feet, and all bodily and spiritual good things, so will you not serve him?

★ XCV ★

A LAYMAN asked Brother Giles to pray to God for him. Go and pray yourself, he answered. Why, since you are able to go, do you stay behind and send someone else in your place? What a thing to say, Brother Giles! I am a sinner, and far removed from God, but you are a friend of God, and can therefore find him quickly on behalf of yourself and others. And the holy man said: Dear brother, if all the squares in Perugia were full of silver and gold, and proclamation were made throughout the city that anyone might help themselves, would you send a messenger to get it for you? Indeed I would not, replied the other. On the contrary, I should go myself and trust no one else, however faithful. Even so is it with God, said Brother Giles. The whole world is filled with him, and everyone can find him. Go yourself, therefore, and do not send somebody else.

★ XCVI ★

It is said that two cardinals once came to Brother
Giles that they might hear from him the words of life.
And as they were about to take their leave, they asked
him to pray for them. He answered: What need is
that I should pray to God for you, seeing that you
have greater faith and hope than I? How so? they said.
Because with so much of riches, honours and worldly
prosperity you still hope to be saved, answered Brother
Giles, whereas I, with so much affliction and adversity,
fear to be damned.

★ XCVII ★

Brother Gratian said to Brother Giles: I can preach
to others and give them advice, and I seem to know
what I ought to do myself. But, being able to do many
things, I cannot tell to what work I ought chiefly to
devote myself, and by so doing please God most. So
give me your advice, and tell me what you think.
Brother Giles answered: There is nothing by which
you would please God more than by hanging yourself.
After Brother Gratian had implored him for many
days to explain what he meant by saying this, Brother
Giles at length gave the following answer: A man
who is hanged is not in heaven, but yet he is raised
above the earth and his eyes are always downcast. Do
the same. Though you are not in heaven, you may still
be raised above earthly things, and in virtuous actions
you may think humbly of yourself and await God's
mercy.

★ XCVIII ★

WHEN BROTHER GILES saw that many liked to preach things which they avoided in practise he would say: It is ten thousand times better for a man to teach himself than to teach the whole world. If you would know much, work much and bow your head much. A noble preacher is Lady Humility. He advised a brother who wanted to preach in the piazza of Perugia to say in his sermon: Boo, Boo; much I talk, but little I do.

★ XCIX ★

A MAN came to Brother Giles and told him that he desired greatly to enter the Order. Brother Giles listened to him and then said: If you will do this, make haste to kill your parents, your brothers and your cousins. The man was dumbfounded by these words and, clasping his hands together, said with tears: O Brother Giles, how could I commit so horrible a crime? What a blockhead you are! said Brother Giles. How can you possibly be such a simpleton? I do not mean that you should kill them with the material sword, but with the mental, for he who does not hate his father and mother cannot be Christ's disciple.

★ C ★

ONCE when Francis was feeling ill and tired, he was obliged to continue his journey on a donkey. His companion, Brother Leonard, who came of noble stock, thought to himself as he trudged along: My family would not even have dreamed of associating with Bernardone, and here am I obliged to accompany his son on foot! Francis, who knew what was passing in his companion's heart, hastily dismounted and said: Here, take my place. It is not at all fitting that you, who are of noble and powerful lineage, should walk whilst I ride. Then Brother Leonard, put to shame by such humility, threw himself at the saint's feet and begged his pardon.

* CI *

WHEN FRANCIS found that his Order was growing fast and that not all who wanted to join were suitable, he described what he expected of them in these words: The perfect friar must be as true to poverty as Bernardo, simple and candid as Leo, chaste as Angelo, intelligent and naturally eloquent as Masseo; he must have a mind fixed on things above, like Giles; his prayer must be like that of Rufino, who is always at prayer, whether awake or asleep, for his mind is always with God; he must be as patient as Brother Juniper, strong in soul and body as John de Laudibus, loving as Roger, and like Brother Lucidus, he must not settle in any place, for when Lucidus has been more than a month in one place and finds he is becoming attached to it, he leaves it at once, saying: Our home is in heaven.

* CII *

THE POPE tried to persuade St Clare to moderate her extreme mortifications and offered to absolve her

85

from her vow of rigorous poverty. Absolve me from my sins, Holy Father, she replied, but not from my wish to follow Christ.

THE PEOPLE came to honour Francis so greatly on account of his holiness that they would kiss not only his hands but even his feet. Some friars were scandalized, and one of them rebuked him, saying: Brother, aren't you aware of what is happening? Don't you see what they are doing? The people are worshipping you, and yet you don't make any attempt to stop them, but seem rather to enjoy it! But Francis was in no way put out and replied: These people never do anything out of reverence for him whom they ought to reverence! This remark only horrified the friar still further. Then Francis said to him: Look, Brother. All this reverence which is paid to me I never take to myself, but simply pass it all on to God. As for me, I keep myself in the dust of humility and give all honour to God. But the people benefit from it; it is God whom they are really worshipping, though they see him only in his creatures.

FRANCIS suffered greatly from an infirmity of the eyes and was told by a physician that it could be relieved by having the veins cauterized. Whilst the iron was being heated, Francis desired to keep up his spirits by addressing the fire in these words: My Brother Fire, noble and useful among all created things, be courteous to me now, for I have always loved you and shall continue to do so for the sake of him who created you. I pray our Creator, who made you, to temper your heat now, so that I can bear it. And when he had said this, he made the sign of the cross over the fire. The brothers who were with him were so moved by compassion that they all fled, and only the physician remained. When the cauterization had been done, they returned and Francis said: Faint-hearts and men of little faith! Why did you run away? I tell you in truth that I felt no pain whatever, and no heat from the fire. And if it is not well done, let it be cauterized again!

⋆ CV ⋆

WHILST convalescing in the garden of St Clare's convent after a grave illness, Francis composed this *Canticle of the Sun*:

Praise be to thee above, Most High, for all thy creatures,
Especially for Brother Sun who brings us the day and sheds his light on us;
Lovely is he, and radiant with great splendour,
And he speaks to us of thee, O Most High.
Praise be to thee, my Lord, for Sister Moon and the Stars
Whom thou has set in the heavens, bright, precious and fair.
Praise be to thee, my Lord, for Brother Wind,

For air and cloud, for calm and all weather
By which thou sustaineth life in all thy creatures.
Praise be to thee, oh Lord, for Sister Water,
Who is useful and humble, precious and pure.
Praise be to thee, my Lord, for Brother Fire,
By whom thou lightest the night;
He is fair and merry, mighty and strong.
Praise be to Thee, my Lord, for our sister Mother Earth
Who sustains and governs us
And brings forth varied fruits, bright flowers and
      plants.
Praise and bless my Lord, and thank and serve him
      with great humility.

★ CVI ★

WHEN he had composed his *Canticle of the Sun*,
Francis wished to send for Brother Pacifico, who had
been known before his conversion as the King of Verse
and was a master of courtly song. Francis wanted him
to take some friars and go through the world preaching
and singing the praises of the Lord. He said that the
best preacher among them should start by preaching
to the people, and after the sermon they should all
together sing the praises of the Lord, as minstrels of
God. And when they had finished singing, the preacher
was to say to the people: We are minstrels of the Lord,
and as our reward we ask that you should show true
penitence. And Francis said: What are the servants of
God but his minstrels who should lift up the hearts of
men and move them to spiritual joy?

SOURCES OF THE QUOTATIONS

Some of the quotations—the Canticle to Brother Sun, and one or two extracts from his letters, *Testament*, and Rule—are from the writings of St Francis himself. Most, however, are recorded by those who knew him or his closest companions. Many are taken from the two versions of his *Life* written by Thomas of Celano, his first biographer. Much of the most picturesque and authentic material was contributed, in one form or another, by Brother Leo, the saint's intimate disciple and secretary. Two collections—*The Mirror of Perfection* and the widely popular *Little Flowers of St Francis*—have been particularly drawn upon. As many of the best-known stories and sayings are to be found in differing versions, the extracts given here have sometimes been freely rendered or condensed. Several fuller translations of the texts are available in English, including the following:

The First and Second Life of St Francis, Thomas of Celano, tr., A. G. Ferrers Howell, London 1908.

The Legend of the Three Companions. Temple Classics 1905.

The Mirror of Perfection, in *St Francis of Assisi—His Life and Writings*, tr., L. Sherley-Price, 1959.

The Life by St Bonaventure, together with the *Mirror of Perfection*, and *The Little Flowers*, Everyman Library 1910.

The Little Flowers of St Francis, tr., L. Sherley-Price, Penguin 1959.

St Francis of Assisi—Legends and Lauds, selected by
 Otto Karrer, tr., N. Wydenbruck, London 1947.
The Writings of St Francis of Assisi, tr., Benen Fahy,
 1963.
A New Fioretti, from unpublished sources, tr., J. R. H.
 Moorman, 1946.
*St Francis of Assisi: Writings and Early Biographies—
 English Omnibus of the Sources for the Life of St
 Francis*, ed. Marion Habig, Chicago 1973.